W9-ASR-786

DATE DUE

The Wild World of Animals

Beavers

Big-Toothed Builders

by Jody Sullivan

Consultant:
Marsha A. Sovada, Ph.D.
Research Wildlife Biologist
Northern Prairie Wildlife Research Center
U.S. Geological Survey

Bridgestone Books
an imprint of Capstone Press
Mankato, Minnesota

C 1   2003   13.95

Bridgestone Books are published by Capstone Press
151 Good Counsel Drive, P.O. Box 669, Mankato, Minnesota 56002
http://www.capstone-press.com

Library of Congress Cataloging-in-Publication Data
Sullivan, Jody.
    Beavers : big-toothed builders / by Jody Sullivan.
    p. cm.— (The wild world of animals)
    Includes bibliographical references (p. 24) and index.
    Summary: An introduction to the physical characteristics, habitat, and behavior
of beavers.
    ISBN 0-7368-1392-6 (hardcover)
    1. Beavers—Juvenile literature. [1. Beavers.] I. Title. II. Series.
QL737.R632 S85 2003
599.37—dc21
                                                                    2001008148

Editorial Credits
Megan Schoeneberger, editor; Karen Risch, product planning editor; Linda Clavel,
    designer; Kelly Garvin, photo researcher

Photo Credits
Ann & Rob Simpson, cover
Corbis (texture), cover, 2, 3, 6, 8, 10, 12, 20, 22, 23, 24
Corbis/W. Perry Conway, 20
Erwin and Peggy Bauer, 4, 14
Frederick D. Atwood, 10
Joe McDonald, 12
PhotoDisc, Inc., 1
Tom and Pat Leeson, 6, 16, 18
Tom Boyden, 8

Table of Contents

tail

claws

4

Beavers

Beavers have thick, waterproof fur. They have wide, flat tails. Their front teeth are long and sharp. The webbed toes on their back feet help them swim. Long claws on their front feet help them dig. Adult beavers can be 4 feet (1.2 meters) long, including the tail.

webbed
connected by pieces of skin

A beaver's coat has two types of fur. Short, soft underfur keeps a beaver warm, even in icy water. Long, heavy guard hairs protect the underfur.

Beavers Are Mammals

Beavers and other mammals are warm-blooded. Female mammals give birth to live young. The young drink milk from their mother. Beavers are rodents. Mice, hamsters, and squirrels also are rodents. The beaver is the largest rodent in North America.

warm-blooded
having a body temperature that stays the same

FUN FACTS

Many years ago, giant beavers the size of black bears lived in North America. They were 7.5 feet (2.3 meters) long.

A Beaver's Habitat

Beavers need habitats with water and trees. Beavers make their homes near streams, rivers, lakes, and ponds. Most beavers live in the United States and Canada. Some beavers are found in northern Europe and northern Asia.

10

A beaver's lodge has a "secret" entrance. A beaver enters its lodge through an underwater tunnel. The inside of the lodge is above the water.

Beaver Lodges and Dams

Beavers build dome-shaped homes called lodges. Lodges keep beavers safe from predators. Beavers build dams to slow the flow of water around lodges. Beavers use stones, plants, mud, and logs to build their homes. They cut down trees by chewing through the trunks.

predator
an animal that hunts
and eats other animals

Beavers can close their nose and ears under water. Beavers usually stay under water for four or five minutes. But they can hold their breath for about 15 minutes.

What Do Beavers Eat?

Beavers are herbivores. They eat mostly plants. Beavers eat branches and bark from trees. They also eat leaves, stems, and roots from plants in summer. Beavers store sticks and logs near their lodges for winter. They then have food when plants are hard to find.

Mating, Birth, and Families

Male and female beavers usually stay together for life. They mate in winter. Female beavers give birth to two to four young in late spring. Both parents take care of the young. The parents, new litter, and yearlings live together in one lodge.

yearling
an animal that is
1 year old or in the
second year of its life

Kits

Young beavers are called kits. Kits weigh up to 1.5 pounds (.7 kilogram) at birth. They have soft, fluffy fur. They drink their mother's milk for up to three months. Young beavers usually stay with their parents for about two years.

Predators

Beavers have many predators. Coyotes, wolves, and bears hunt beavers. Beavers swim and dive to get away from predators. They slap their tail on the water when they sense danger. This action produces a noise that warns other beavers.

coyote

a wolflike animal that lives throughout much of the United States

In the late 1600s, a person could trade one beaver skin for a cooking pot.

Beavers and People

Some people trap beavers for their fur. American Indians and early settlers used beaver skins as money. They killed thousands of beavers. Beavers almost became extinct in some places. Today, people protect beavers. Beavers can be trapped only at certain times of the year.

extinct
no longer living anywhere in the world

Hands On: Build a Dam

Beavers build dams to slow the flow of water around their lodges. You can build your own dam to see how it works.

What You Need

Pan or tray with high sides
Cork
Plastic pitcher of water or outdoor water faucet with hose
Sticks
Mud

What You Do

1. Do this activity outdoors. Place the pan on the ground so that one end is slightly higher than the other end. Place the cork at the high end.
2. Use a pitcher or hose to gently run water from the high end of the pan. What happens to the cork?
3. Empty the water. Build a dam across the middle of the pan by piling twigs together with mud. Let the mud dry.
4. Place the cork at the high end of the pan. Gently run the water again. What happens to the cork this time?

The cork is like a beaver's lodge. Running water would wash it away. But the dam slows the flow of water and the cork stays in place.

Words to Know

habitat (HAB-uh-tat)—the place where an animal lives

herbivore (HUR-buh-vor)—an animal that eats mostly plants

litter (LIT-ur)—a group of animals born to one mother at one time

lodge (LOJ)—a beaver's home

mammal (MAM-uhl)—a warm-blooded animal that has a backbone and feeds milk to its young

mate (MATE)—to join together to produce young

predator (PRED-uh-tur)—an animal that hunts and eats other animals

rodent (ROHD-uhnt)—a small mammal with long front teeth used for gnawing; mice, squirrels, and beavers are rodents.

Read More

Bauman, Amy, and Patricia Corrigan. *The Wonder of Beavers.* Animal Wonders. Milwaukee: Gareth Stevens, 2000.

Gibson, Deborah Chase. *Beavers and Their Homes.* Animal Habitats. New York: PowerKids Press, 1999.

Internet Sites

Canadian Wildlife Service—Hinterland Who's Who—Beaver

http://www.cws-scf.ec.gc.ca/hww-fap/beaver/beaver.html

Castor Canadensis (Beaver)

http://animaldiversity.ummz.umich.edu/accounts/castor/c._canadensis$narrative.html

Index